SIMPLE
SPEECH

Because you are but a young man, beware of temptations and snares; and above all, be careful to keep yourself in the use of means; resort to good company; and howbeit you be nicknamed a Puritan, and mocked, yet care not for that, but rejoice and be glad, that they who are scorned and scoffed by this godless and vain world, and nicknamed Puritans, would admit you to their society; for I must tell you, when I am at this point as you see me, I get no comfort to my soul by any second means under heaven but from those who are nicknamed Puritans. They are the men that can give a word of comfort to a wearied soul in due season, and that I have found by experience . . .

The Last and Heavenly Speeches, and
Glorious Departure, of John, Viscount Kenmure

SINFUL
SPEECH

John Flavel

Taken from
'A Caution to Seamen: A Dissuasive against
Several Horrid and Detestable Sins',
The Works of John Flavel, Vol. 5
&
'The Reasonableness of Personal Reformation',
The Works of John Flavel, Vol. 6

THE BANNER OF TRUTH TRUST

THE BANNER OF TRUTH TRUST
3 Murrayfield Road, Edinburgh EH12 6EL, UK
P.O. Box 621, Carlisle, PA 17013, USA

*

© The Banner of Truth Trust 2009

ISBN-978 1 84871 017 7

*

Typeset in 10.5 / 13.5 pt Adobe Caslon Pro
at the Banner of Truth Trust, Edinburgh

Printed in the USA by
Versa Press, Inc.,
East Peoria, IL

*

Minor editorial adjustments have been made to the
original text, e.g. the modernizing of some words
and the supplying of Scripture references.

SINFUL SPEECH

THE second evil I shall deal with is the evil of the tongue,[1] which as St James says, is full of deadly poison, oaths, curses, blasphemies; and this poison it scatters up and down the world in all places; an untamed member that none can rule, (*James* 3:7-8). The fiercest of beasts have been tamed by man, as the apostle there observes, which is a relic of his old superiority and dominion over them; but this is an unruly member

[1] For the other evils Flavel deals with see 'A Caution to Seamen: A Dissuasive against Several Horrid and Detestable Sins', *The Works of John Flavel*, vol. 5 (London: Banner of Truth, 1968, oft. repr.), pp. 293-342.

that none can tame but he that made it; no beast so fierce and crabbed as this is. It may be, I may be bitten by it for my labour and endeavours to put a restraint upon it: but I shall adventure it. My design is not to dishonour, or exasperate you; but if my faithfulness to God and you should accidentally do so, I cannot help that.

Friends, Providence oftentimes confines many of you together within the narrow limits of a ship, where you have time enough, and if your hearts were sanctified, many choice advantages of edifying one another. O what transcendent subjects does Providence daily present you with, to take up your discourses! How many experiences of extraordinary mercies and preservations have you to relate to one another, and bless the Lord for! Also, how many works of wonder do you daily behold, who go down into the deeps? O what heavenly employment is here for your tongues! How should they be talking of all his wonders? How should you call upon each other, as David did, 'Come hither, and I will tell you what God hath done for my soul', at such a time, in such an extremity (*Psa.* 66:16)? How should you call upon one another to pay 'the vows your lips have uttered in your distress?' Thus should one provoke another in this angelic work, as one lively bird sets the whole flock a chirping.

But tell me, Sirs, should a man come aboard you at sea, and ask of you as Christ did of those two disciples going to Emmaus, 'What manner of communication is this that you have by the way?' (*Luke* 24:17), O what a sad account would he have from most of you! It may be he should find one *jesting,* and another *swearing,* a third *reviling* godliness, and the professors of it; so that it would be a little hell for a serious Christian to be confined to your society. This is not, I am confident, the manner of all. We have a company of more sober seamen, and blessed be God for them; but surely thus stands the case with most of you. O what stuff is here from persons professing Christianity, and bordering close upon the confines of eternity as you do?

It is not my purpose to write of all the diseases of the tongue; that would fill a volume, and is inconsistent with my intended brevity. Who can recount the evils of the tongue? The apostle says, 'It is a world of iniquity', (*James* 3:6). And if there be a world of sin in one member, who can number the sins of all the members? Laurentius reckons as many sins of the tongue as there are letters in the alphabet. And it is an observable note that one has upon Romans 3:13-14; that when Paul anatomizes the natural man there, he insists longer upon the organs of speech than all the other members; 'Their throat is an open sepulchre, with their tongues they have used deceit: the poison of asps is under their lips, their mouth is full of cursing and bitterness.'

But, to be short, we find the Spirit of God in Scripture comparing the tongue to a tree, 'A wholesome tongue is a tree of life' (*Prov.* 15:4). And words are the fruit of the tree, 'I create the fruit of the lips' (*Isa.* 57:19). Some of these trees bear precious fruits, and it is a lovely sight to behold them laden with them in their seasons, 'A word fitly spoken, is like apples of gold in pictures of silver' (*Prov.* 25:11). Such a tongue is a tree of life. Others of these trees bear evil fruit, grapes of Sodom, and clusters of Gomorrah. I shall only insist upon two sorts of these fruits, namely (1.) Withered, sapless fruit; I mean idle and unprofitable words. (2.) Rotten and corrupt fruit; I mean, profane oaths, and profanations of the sacred name of God. No fruit in the world is so apt to corrupt and taint as the fruit of the lips. When it is so, the Scripture calls it σαπρος λογος, 'corrupt' or 'rotten communication' (*Eph.* 4:29).

To prevent this the Spirit of God prescribes an excellent way to season our words, and keep them sweet and sound, that they may neither wither nor become idle and sapless, or putrify and become rotten, as profane words are, 'Let your speech be always with grace, seasoned with salt, that you may know how to answer every man' (*Col.* 4:6). Oh! if the salt of grace were once cast into the fountain, the heart-streams must necessarily become more savoury and pleasant, as the waters of Marah when they were healed (cf. *Exod.* 15:23-25). My present work is to attempt the cure of this double evil of *idle words* and *profane oaths*, whereof thousands among you are deeply guilty. I shall begin with the first, *viz.* idle words.

1. Idle Words.

That is, useless chat, unprofitable talk, that is not referred any way to the glory of God.
This is a common evil, and little

regarded by most men; but yet a sin of severer aggravations than most imagine: light words weigh heavy in God's balance.

Argument i.

For, first, The evil of them is exceedingly aggravated by this: they abuse and pervert the tongue, that noble member, from that employment and use which God by the law of creation designed it to.

God gave not to man the organs and power of speech, (which is his excellency above the beasts) to serve a passion or vain humour, to vent the froth and vanity of his spirit; but to extol the Creator, and render him the praise of all his admirable and glorious works. For though the creation be a curious well-tuned instrument, yet man is the musician that must touch it, and make the melody. This was the end of God in forming those instruments and organs: but now hereby they are subject to Satan and lust, and employed to the dishonour of God who made them. God is pleased to suspend the power of speech (as we see in children) until reason begins to bud in them: they have not the liberty of one, until they have the use of the other; which plainly shows, that God is not willing to have our words run waste.

Argument 2.

It is a sinful wasting of our precious time; and that puts a further aggravation upon it.

Consider, sirs, the time of life is but a little spot between two eternities. The long-suffering God wheels about those glorious celestial bodies over your heads in a constant revolution to beget time for you; and the preciousness of every minute thereof results from its use and end: it is intended and afforded as a space to you to repent in (*Rev.* 2:21). And therefore great things depend upon it: no less than your eternal happiness or misery hangs upon those precious opportunities. Every minute of it has an influence into eternity. How would the damned value one hour of it if they might enjoy it! The business you have to do in it is of unspeakable weight and concern: this great work, this soul-work, and eternity-work, lies upon your hands; you are cast into straits of time about it: and, if so, what an evil is it in you to waste it away thus to no purpose!

ARGUMENT 3.

It is a sin that few are sensible of as they are of other sins, and therefore the more dangerous.

It is commonly committed, and that without checks of conscience. Other sins, as murder and adultery, though they be horrid sins, yet are but seldom committed, and when they are, conscience is startled at the horridness of them; few, except they be prodigious wretches indeed, dare make light of them. But now for idle and vain words, there are innumerable swarms of these every day, and few regard them. The intercourse between the heart and tongue is quick; they are quickly committed, and as easily forgotten.

Argument 4.

And then, fourthly, They have mischievous effects upon others.

How long does an idle word, or foolish jest, stick in men's minds, and become an occasion of much sin to them? The froth and vanity of your spirit, which your tongue so freely vents among your vain companions, may be working in their minds when you are in the dust, and so be transmitted from one to another; for unto that no more is requisite than an *objective existence* of those vain words in their memories. And thus may you be sinning in the persons of your companions, when you are turned into dust.

And this is one reason that Suarez gives for a general judgment, after men have passed their particular judgment immediately after their death, 'Because, (says he) after this, multitudes of sins by their means will be committed in the world, for which they must yet be judged to a fuller measure of wrath.' So that look as many of the precious servants of God, now in glory, have left many weighty and holy sayings behind them, by which many thousands of souls have been benefited, and God glorified on earth, after they had left it: so you leave that vanity upon the minds of others behind you, by which he may be dishonoured to many generations.

And then, for profane oaths:

11. Profane Oaths

For profane oaths are the corrupt fruit of a graceless heart.

Oh! how common are these among you? Yea, the habit of swearing is so strengthened in some, that they have lost all sense and conscience of the sin. Now, oh! that I might prevail with you to repent of this wickedness, and break the force of this customary evil among you! Will you but give me the reading of a few pages more, and weigh with the reason of men, what you read? If you will not hearken to counsel, it is a fatal sign, (2 *Cor.* 2:15-16), and you shall mourn for this obstinacy hereafter, (*Prov.* 5:12-13). Desperate is that evil that scorns the remedy. And if you have patience to read it, the Lord give you an heart to consider what you read, and obey the counsels of God; or else it were better your eyes had never seen these lines. Well, then, I beseech you consider,

Argument 1.

That profane oaths are an high abuse of the dreadful and sacred name of God, which should neither be spoken nor thought of without the deepest awe and reverence. It is the taking of that sacred name in vain (Exod. 20:7).

Now God is exceeding tender and jealous over his name; it is dear to him; his name is dreadful and glorious; 'I am a great king, and my name is dreadful among the heathen' (*Mal.* 1:14).

The heathens would not ordinarily mention the names of such as they reverenced.

Suetonius says that Augustus prohibited the common use of his name: he thought it an indignity to have his name tossed up and down in everyone's mouth. Yea, says Dr Willet on Exodus 20, it was an use among them to keep secret such names as they would have in reverence. They dared not mention the name of Demogorgon, whom they held to be the first god: they thought when he was named, the earth would tremble. Also the name of Mercurius Tresmegistus was very sparingly used because of that reverence the people had for him.

Now, consider, shall poor worms be so tender of preserving the reverence of their names! Shall not heathens dare to use the names of their idols; and shall the sacred and dreadful name of the true God be thus bandied up and down by tongues of his own creatures? Will not God be avenged for these abuses of his name? Be confident, it shall one day be sanctified upon you in judgment, because you did not sanctify it according to your duty.

ARGUMENT 2.

Swearing is a part of the worship of God; and therefore profane swearing can be no less than the profanation of his worship, and robbing him of all the glory he has thereby.

'Thou shalt fear the LORD thy God, and serve him, and shalt swear by his name' (*Deut.* 6:13). So Jeremiah 4:2: 'Thou shalt swear the LORD liveth, in truth, in judgment, and in righteousness.' If a man swear by God after this manner, God is exceedingly glorified thereby. Now, that you may see what revenue of glory God has from this part of his worship, and how it becomes a part of Divine worship, you must know then an oath is nothing else but the *asking or desiring a Divine testimony for the confirmation of the truth of our testimony:* 'For men verily swear by the greater; and an oath for confirmation is to them an end of all strife' (*Heb.* 6:16). The corruption of human nature by the fall has made man such a false and fickle creature, that his single testimony cannot be sufficient security for another especially in weighty cases, to rest upon; and therefore in swearing, he calls God for a witness of the truth of what he affirms, or promises: I say, calls God to be a witness of the truth of what he says, because he is *truth* itself, and cannot lie (*Heb.* 6:18).

Now this calling for, or asking of a testimony from God, makes an oath become a part of God's worship, and gives him a great deal of glory and honour; for hereby he that swears acknowledges his *omniscience* and *infallible truth* and *righteousness*. His *omniscience* is acknowledged: for by this appeal to him, we imply and acknowledge him to be the 'Searcher of the heart and mind' (cf. *Psa.* 26:2); that he knows the secret intents and meaning of our spirits.

His supreme and infallible truth is also acknowledged; for this is manifestly carried in an oath, that though I am a false and deceitful creature, and my affirmation cannot obtain universal and full credence, yet he that is greater than I, by whose name I swear, cannot deceive.

And, lastly, his *righteousness* is acknowledged in an oath: for he that swears does, either *expressly* or *implicitly*, put himself under the curse and wrath of God, if he swear falsely. Every oath has an execration or imprecation in it, 'They entered into a curse, and an oath, to walk in God's law' (*Neh.* 10:29). And so 2 Corinthians 1:23: 'I call God for a record upon my soul.' And the usual form in the Old Testament was, 'The Lord do so to me, and more also.'

Now hereby God has the glory of his righteousness and justice given him by the creature, and therefore it is a choice part of the divine worship, or of that homage which a creature owes to his God. And if this be so, then how easily may the sin of rash and profane oaths be hence argued and aggravated? The more excellent any thing is by an institution of God, by so much more horrid and abominable is the abuse thereof.

O how often is the dreadful Majesty of heaven and earth called to witness to frivolous things, and oft to be a witness of our rage and fury! (cf. 1 *Sam.* 14:39). Is it a light thing to rob him of his peculiar glory, and subject poor souls to his curse and wrath, who has said, 'He will be a swift witness against you' (*Mal.* 3:5)? Your tongues are nimble in committing this sin, and God will be swift in punishing it.

ARGUMENT 3.

It is a sin which God has severely threatened to punish and that with temporal and corporal plagues.

'For by reason of oaths, the land mourns' (*Hos.* 4:2-3). That is, it brings the heavy judgment of God upon whole nations, under which they shall mourn. And in Zechariah 5:2-4, you have there a 'roll of curses'; i.e. a catalogue of judgments and woes, 'the length thereof twenty cubits' (i.e. ten yards); to set out the multitude of woes contained in it: it is a long catalogue, and a 'flying roll', to denote the *swiftness* of it: it flies towards the house of the swearer; it makes haste. The judgments that are written in it linger not, but are even in pain to be delivered. And this flying roll, full of dreadful woes, flies and enters into the house of the swearer; 'and it shall therein remain', says the Lord; it shall cleave to his family; none shall claw off these woes from him: and it shall consume the timber thereof, and the stones thereof, i.e. bring utter subversion, ruin, and desolation to his house.

O dreadful sin! what a desolation it makes! Your mouths are full of oaths, and your houses shall be full of curses. Woe to that wretched family, into which this flying roll shall enter! Woe, I say, to the wretched inhabitants thereof! 'The curse of the LORD (says Solomon) is in the house of the wicked; but he blesseth the habitation of the just' (*Prov.* 3:33). *Tuguriolum,* i.e. (says Mercer) *his poor little tenement or cottage.* There is a blessing, the promises, like clouds of blessing, dwell over it, and drop mercies on it; but a curse in the house of the wicked.

Ah! how many stately mansions are there, in which little other language but oaths and curses are heard! And these are as so much gun-powder laid under the foundation of them, which, when justice shall set fire to, O what work will it make! Woe to the inhabitants thereof! Well then, break off this sin by repentance, unless you intend to ruin your families, and bring all the curses of God into your houses. If you have no pity for yourselves, yet pity your posterity; have mercy for your wives and children; do not ruin all for the indulgence of a lust.

ARGUMENT 4.

But that is not all; it brings soul-judgments and spiritual plagues upon you: it brings hell along with it.

And if you be not afraid to sin, yet I think, you should be afraid to *burn:* if the love of God can work nothing upon your brawny heart, yet, I think, the terrors of the Lord should startle and frighten it. To this purpose, I beseech you to weigh these scriptures; and I think, unless God has lost all his authority with you, and hell all its terrors, it should startle you.

The first is that dreadful scripture, James 5:12: 'But above all things, my brethren, swear not; neither by heaven, neither by the earth, neither by any other oath, but let your yea be yea; and your nay, nay; lest ye fall into condemnation.'

Mark, *above all things,* a form of vehemency and earnestness, like that, Ephesians 6:16: 'But above all, taking the shield of faith'. As faith has a prelation there before all the graces, so swearing here before all other vices. 'Swear not', i.e. *vainly, rashly, profanely;* for otherwise it is a lawful thing, and a part of God's worship, as I have shown: but swear not vain oaths, by the creatures, heaven, or earth, &c. which is to advance the creature into the room of God: a sin to which the Jews were much addicted. But, 'let your yea, be yea; and your nay, nay'; i.e. accustom yourselves to short and plain affirmations and negations, to a simple and candid expression of your minds. And the thundering argument that backs it, is this, 'lest ye fall into condemnation'; i.e. lest for these things the Judge of heaven and earth pass a sentence of condemnation to hell upon you.

O sirs! dare you touch this hot iron? Dare you from henceforth commit that sin, that you know will bring you under the condemnation and judgment of God? Do you know what it is for a soul to be cast at God's bar? Did you never see a poor malefactor tried at the assizes, and observe how his face gathers paleness, how his legs tremble, and death displays its colours in his cheeks, when sentence is given upon him? But what is that to God's condemnation? What is a gallows to hell?

Another text I would recommend to your consideration is Exodus 20:7: 'The LORD will not hold him guiltless that taketh his name in vain'; where vain oaths are especially included.

Now, what does God mean, when he says, he will not hold him guiltless? The meaning is plain, his sins shall be reckoned and imputed to him; they shall lie upon his soul; he shall be bound over to answer to God for them. O terrible sentence! What soul can bear it, or stand before it! 'Blessed is the man (says David) to whom the LORD imputeth not iniquity': surely then, cursed is that man to whom God will impute them: and to the swearer they shall all be imputed, if he break not off his sin by repentance, and get a Christ the sooner.

Oh, how dare you think of going before the Lord with the guilt of all your sins upon you? When Christ would administer the very spirit of joy into one sentence to a poor sinner, he said, 'Son, be of good cheer, your sins be forgiven' (*Matt.* 9:2). And when God would contract the sum of all misery into one word, he says, 'His sins shall lie down with him in the dust', (*Job* 20:11). Ah, soul! one of these days you shall be laid on your death-bed, or see the waves that shall entomb you, leaping and roaring upon every side; and then you will surely have other thoughts of the happiness that lies in remission of sin than you have now.

Observe the most incorrigible sinner then; hear how he sighs and groans, and cries, Ah, Lord! and must I die? And then see how the tears trickle down his cheeks, and his heart ready to burst within him. Why, what is the matter? Oh! the Lord will not pardon him, he holds him guilty! If he were sure his sins were forgiven, then he could die: but, oh! to appear before the Lord in them, appals him, daunts him, kills the very heart of him! He would happily cry for mercy, but conscience stops his mouth. O, says conscience, how can you move that tongue to God in prayer for mercy, that has so often rent and torn his glorious name, by oaths and curses?

Flavel on Sinful Speech 33

Sirs, I pray you do not make light of these things; they will look wishfully upon you one of these days, except you prevent it by sound conversion.

ARGUMENT 5.

And then, lastly, to name no more, I pray you consider, that a custom of vain words and profane oaths is as plain an indication and discovery of an unregenerate soul as any in the world.

This is a sure sign you are none of Christ's, nor have anything to do with the promises and privileges of his people; for by this the Scripture distinguishes the state of saints and sinners, 'There is one event to the righteous, and to the wicked; to the clean and to the unclean; to him that sacrificeth, and to him that sacrificeth not: as is the good, so is the sinner: and he that sweareth, as he that feareth an oath' (*Eccles.* 9:2). Mark, he that swears, and he that fears an oath, do as manifestly distinguish the children of God from wicked men, as clean and unclean, righteous and wicked, sacrificing and not sacrificing. The fruit of the tongue plainly shows what the tree is that bears it: 'The vile person will speak villany' (*Isa.* 32:6); and 'out of the abundance of the heart the mouth speaks' (*Luke* 6:45). *Loquere, ut videam,* said one: 'Speak, that I may see what you are.' Look, what is in the heart is vented by the tongue; where the treasures of grace are in the heart, words ministering grace will be in the lips: 'The mouth of the righteous speaketh wisdom, and his tongue talketh of judgment; for the law of the LORD is in his heart' (*Psa.* 37:30-31).

To this sense we must understand that scripture, 'By thy words thou shalt be justified, and by thy words thou shalt be condemned' (*Matt.* 12:37). Certainly justification and condemnation, in the day of judgment shall not pass upon us merely for the good or bad words we have spoken; but according to the state of the person and frame of the heart. But the meaning is, that our words shall justify or condemn us in that day, as evidence of the state and frame of the soul. We use to say, such witnesses hanged a man; the meaning is, the evidence they gave cast and condemned him.

O think seriously of this; if words evidence the state of the soul, what a woeful state must your soul necessarily be in, whose mouth overflows with oaths and curses! How many witnesses will be brought in to cast you in the great day? 'Your own tongue shall then fall upon you', as the expression is in Psalm 64:8. And out of your own mouth God will fetch abundant evidence to condemn you.

And thus I have opened unto you the evil of vain words and profane oaths; and presented to your view their several aggravations. If by these things there be a relenting pang upon your heart, and a serious resolution of reformation, then I shall recommend these few helps or means to your perusal, and conclude this head.

Seriously fix in your thoughts that scripture, 'But I say unto you, that every idle word that men shall speak, they shall give an account thereof in the day of judgment' (Matt. 12:36).

O let it sound in your ears day and night! O ponder them in your heart! *I say unto you,* I that have always been in the Father's bosom, and do fully know his mind, that I am constituted the Judge of quick and dead, and do fully understand the rule of judgment, and the whole process thereof, I say, and do assure you, that 'every idle word that men shall speak', i.e., every word that has not a tendency and reference to the glory of God, though there be no other obliquity of evil in them than this, that they lack a good end; how much more then, scurrilous words, bloody oaths, and blasphemies? *Men shall give an account thereof;* that is, shall be cast and condemned to suffer the wrath of God for them; as appears by that parallel scripture, 1 Peter 4:4-5. For as the learned observe, there is plainly a *metalepsis* in these words; *the antecedent to give an account,* is put for the *consequent,* punishment, and condemnation to hell-fire: the certainty whereof admits but of this one exception, *viz.* intervenient repentance, or pardon obtained through the blood of Christ here before you be presented at that judgment-seat.

O then, what a bridle should this text be to your extravagant tongue! I remember Jerome often said, 'Whether I eat or drink, or whatever I do, I think I still hear the sound of these words in my ear, "Arise, you dead, and come to judgment.'" O that the sound of these words may be always in your ears!

HELP 2.

Consider before you speak, and be not rash to utter words without knowledge.

He that speaks what he thinks not, speaks *hypocritically;* and he that thinks not what to speak, speaks *inconsiderately.* You have cause to weigh your words before you deliver them by your tongue; for whether you do, or do not, the Lord *ponders* them: records are kept of them, else you could not be called to an account for them, as I showed you, you must.

Help 3.

Resign up your tongue to God every day, and beg him to guide and keep it.

So did David, 'Set a watch, O LORD, before my mouth, and keep the door of my lips' (*Psa.* 141:3). Beg him to keep you from provocations and temptations; or, if you fall into them, intreat him for strength to rule your spirits in them, that you may not be conquered by temptations.

Help 4.

But above all, labour to get your souls cleansed and purified by faith, possessed with saving and gracious principles: all other means will be ineffectual without this.

O see the vileness of your nature, and

the necessity of a change to pass upon it! First make the tree good, and then his fruit good: a new nature will produce new words and actions. To bind your souls with vows and resolutions, while you are strangers to a regenerate work, is to bind Samson with green willow twigs, whilst his locks remain upon his head.

I will conclude with the advice of that divine poet, Mr George Herbert; it may be, it may affect you, and run in your thoughts when you are alone.

Take not his name, who made thy mouth, in vain;
   It gets thee nothing, and hath no excuse.
Lust and wine plead a pleasure; avarice gain:
   But the cheap swearer, through his open sluice,
     Lets his soul run nought, as little fearing.
     Were I an Epicure, I could hate swearing.

When thou dost tell another's jest, therein
  Omit the oaths which true wit cannot need:
Pick out of tales the mirth, but not the sin.
  He pares the apple that will cleanly feed.
    Play not away the virtue of that name,
    Which is thy best stake when grief makes thee tame.

The cheapest sins most dearly punish'd are,
  Because to shun them also is so cheap;
For we have wit to mark them, and to spare
  O crumble not away thy soul's fair heap.
    If thou wilt die, the gates of hell are broad,
    Pride and full sins have made the way a road.

The following is taken from
'The Reasonableness of Personal Reformation',
The Works of John Flavel, Vol. 6.

*I*n *this chapter the true censure and judgment of right reason and conscience, are given upon profane swearing, and blaspheming the name of God: as also their replies to several pleas offered in defence or excuse thereof.*

1. *God bestowed on man the noble faculty of speech, (a peculiar favour and privilege) for two ends and uses.*

(1) That by the use of his tongue, he may glorify his Maker, and sound forth the praises of his Redeemer.

(2) That we might thereby be able to communicate our minds one to another, in all our necessary and convenient interests and concerns, whether civil or religious.

This member, (the tongue) though small in quantity, is found to be mighty in efficacy; and whilst it is kept under the rule and government of grace, the words that drop from it, are as apples of gold in pictures of silver. Gracious words are bread to feed, and water to refresh the souls of others. A sanctified tongue is as a tree of life. Conversion, edification, and consolation, are the delicious fruits of the lips.

But the tongues of some men break loose from under all the laws and rules both of reason and religion, and serve only to vent the froth and filth, which abound in the heart, as in a fountain of pollution: 'for out of the abundance of the heart, the mouth speaks.' The tongue moves lightly, but falls heavily; it strikes soft, but wounds deep. It would not spare men of the highest rank and eminence, did not the fear of capital punishments teach them so much wit, to keep their tongues in prison, that they may keep their bodies out of prison. And though, for this reason, they are afraid of making too bold with the names of men; yet having no fear of God at all, they fall upon his great and dreadful name, tossing it to and fro, without any respect or reverence.

Augustus prohibited the common use of his name, lest it should grow too cheap and vile, by the common and needless using of it. The name of Mercurius Trismegistus was very sparingly used, because of the great reverence the people had for him. The very heathens were afraid to pronounce the name of their great god, Demogorgon, as fearing the earth would tremble, when his name was mentioned. How does the reverence of heathens to their false gods, expose and aggravate the impudence of professed Christians, in their vile indignities and abuses of the great and terrible name of the true God! Yea, they not only take up his name vainly and rashly into their lips, but audaciously insert it by a profane oath into their common talk, as that which gives the grace, wit, and ornament to their discourses. Some have not been ashamed to say, what pity is it, that swearing should be a sin, which gives so great a grace and ornament to language?

2. *Swearing by the name of God in a righteous cause, when called thereto by due authority, is not only a lawful, but a religious act, founded upon, and directed to the honour of God's omniscience; whereunto there is a solemn appeal made, in every assertory and promissory oath, and a religious acknowledgment made him, of his infallible knowledge of the truth or falsehood of our hearts, and all the secrets of them, be they never so involved and inward things.*

The lawful use and end of swearing, is to put an end to all strife, and to maintain both equity and charity among men—the two bonds and ligaments of human society.

Now, it being the sovereign right and property of God alone, infallibly to *search and try the hearts and minds of men*, he thereby becomes the infallible witness to the truth or falsehood of what they speak; so that in every such lawful oath, there is not only a solemn appeal, and in that appeal an ascription of glory to his sovereign omniscience; but therein (implicitly at least) they put themselves under his wrath and curse, in case they swear falsely; which makes this action most sacred and solemn.

The deep corruption of human nature by the fall, makes these appeals to God under a curse necessary. For it is supposed, though men be false and deceitful, yet there is some reverence of a deity, and fear of his wrath and curse, left unextinguished in their fallen nature. So that men will rather speak the truth (though to their own shame and loss) than by invoking so glorious a name in vain, put both soul and body under his wrath and curse.

By which it appears what an awful and solemn thing an oath is; and that every good man, not only takes a lawful oath with holy fear and trembling, because of the solemnity of the action; but rather ought to choose death, than to swear profanely, because of the horrid malignity of the action.

3. *The insult and malignity found in profane oaths, appears in that terrible threatening, 'The LORD will not hold him guiltless that taketh his name in vain': a threatening, altogether as just and righteous as it is severe and terrible.*

This sin admits of degrees of guilt. It is highly sinful to swear by the name of God lightly and vainly in our common discourses, though the oath be clipped, and half suppressed, or disguised in the pronunciation of it; which argues the remains of fear and shame in the sinner.

It is yet worse (and indeed not a jot below blasphemy) to swear by any other name, than the name of God: for in so doing, they attribute to a creature the sovereign and incommunicable property of God, set that creature in the very throne of God, and invest it with the regalities of his omniscience, to know our hearts, and almighty power, to avenge the wrong upon us, done to himself, as well as to men, by false swearing.

But to break in rudely and blasphemously upon the sacred and tremendous name of God, with bold and full-mouthed oaths, striking through his sacred name with direct insulting blasphemies; this argues an heart, from which all fear of God is utterly expelled and banished.

Yet some there are, grown up to that prodigious height of impiety, that they dare assault the very heavens, and discharge whole volleys of blasphemies against the glorious majesty which dwells there. They are not afraid to bid defiance to him, and challenge the God who made them, to do his worst. They deck and adorn (as they account it) their common discourse with bloody oaths, and horrid imprecations; not reckoning them genteel and modish without them. It consists not with the greatness of their spirits, to be wicked at the common rate. They are willing to let the world know, that they are none of those puny, silly fellows, that are afraid of invisible powers, or so much cowards, as to slip a full-mouthed oath, by suppressing, or whispering the emphatical sounding syllable; but think an horrid blasphemy makes the most sweet and graceful cadency in their hellish rhetoric. They glory, that they have fully conquered all those troublesome notions of good and evil, virtue and vice, heaven and hell, to that degree, that they can now affront the divine Majesty to his very face, and not fear the worst he threatens in his word against their wickedness.

If there be a God, (which they scarce believe) they are resolved, audaciously to provoke him to give them a convincing evidence of his being. And if he be (as they are told he is) rich in patience and forbearance, they are resolved to try how far his patience will extend, and what load of wickedness it is capable of bearing.

If their damnation be not yet sure enough, they will do their utmost to make it sure, by breaking down the only bridge whereby they can escape damnation: I mean, by trampling under their feet the precious blood and wounds of the Son of God, and imprecating the damnation of hell upon their own souls, as if it slumbered too long, and were too slow-paced in its motions towards them. I am of opinion, there are few Christians to be found on earth, crying so often, *Lord, pardon; Lord save me;* as some wretches among us cry, (I tremble to speak it!) *God damn me: the devil take me.*

Herein they seem to envy the happiness of the devils, and damned wretches in hell, and endeavour (as one speaks) to snatch damnation out of God's hand before the time; as if they could not be soon enough among their roaring and howling companions in the midst of the everlasting burnings. But, why such haste to be perfectly miserable? The very devils themselves deprecate torments before their time, though you imprecate them. Your misery makes haste enough towards you; you need not quicken it, or thus run to meet it.

I am persuaded, that if the bars of the bottomless pit were broken up, and devils should ascend in human shapes, none among them would be found hastening upon themselves the fulness and completeness of their misery, as you do. It is a truth, though a strange one, that it is much easier to find, than imagine men upon earth professing Christian religion, yet in some respect sunk below the wickedness of the diabolical nature, by making damnation both the subject of their jesting and the object of their very wishes and desires. Some greater masters of our language, may more lively and emphatically express the horrid nature of this sin; but excuse me, reader, if I believe no words or thoughts can measure the height or depth of this monstrous abomination.

4. *Such insulting language as this (especially when grown modish, or common) cannot but be a most high and dreadful provocation of God, and such an one as will certainly bring down his desolating vengeance, not only upon the heads of blasphemers themselves, but upon the states and kingdoms that connive at, or tolerate them.*

We read of a flying roll full of curses, the length thereof twenty cubits, and the breadth thereof ten cubits; which shall enter into the house of the swearer, remain in the midst of his house, and consume it with the timber and stones thereof (*Zech.* 5:2-4).

Blasphemy and profane swearing are like barrels of gunpowder laid under the foundation of many great and noble families, many of which are already blown up, and laid in ruins by this sin, and many more are ready to follow, as soon as the justice of God shall give fire to it.

And (comparatively speaking) it were happy if the mischief ended here; but, alas! it causes God to commence a quarrel with the whole land; 'And because of oaths, the land mourneth' (*Hos.* 4:2-3). You find in

Isaiah 3:8 what it was that brought that unparalleled desolation upon that famous and flourishing city of Jerusalem, and the whole land of Judah; 'for Jerusalem is ruined, and Judah is fallen; because their tongues and their doings are against the LORD, to provoke the eyes of his glory.'

But, alas! scripture-threatenings signify scarce so much with these men, as the predictions of the weather in an almanack; and, which is strange to consider, the very execution of scripture-threatenings before their eyes, will not terrify them from this inhuman wickedness; even these also are laughed to scorn, or easily forgotten.

O! that God would set it home with power, upon the spirits of all that are in power, to take some speedy and effectual course to remove this accursed thing, this iniquity to be punished by the judge; one (and a chief one too) of those direful provocations of heaven, to which we owe a special part of our national infelicity at this day. We all acknowledge, that all prosperity and success depends upon God; if so, reason will readily own, that it must be therefore the interest of kingdoms and commonwealths to prevent and restrain those impieties, which so audaciously provoke and incense his wrath. As much is this their duty and interest, as it is the interest of a courtier to avoid offences of his royal master, the king, upon whose favour his honour and preferment depends: or as it is the duty of the owner, to keep in that ox which is used to goring, or cover that pit into which some have, and others of his family are like to fall: or carefully and speedily to remove that gunpowder, which his enemies have placed under the foundation of his house, to blow it up. Both reason and experience will inform the rulers of this world, that professed rebels to the God of heaven, are never like to make useful subjects in the kingdom of men.

5. *Until public justice lay hold upon such offenders, let us try what close reasoning may effect, for their reformation.*

It is hard to imagine that men of sense should so generally, and so far engage themselves in this course of profane swearing, and have nothing at all to say for themselves.

If they have no reason at all, to offer in justification or excuse of what they do, they act the brutes, not the men, and are self-condemned already.

It is a question with me, whether the soul of man, on this side of hell, can sink so deep into the nature of a devil, as to sin because he will sin; or to engage himself in a course of sin, without any respect at all to some carnal interest, either of profit, pleasure, or honour?

The thief has a visible temptation of gain to allure him, or pinching necessity, to induce him. The liar is drawn in, to commit that second sin, to cover the shame and turpitude of a former. The adulterer promises himself pleasure in the satisfaction of his lusts. And though men generally stand amazed to think, what that temptation should be, which prevails upon the swearer; yet doubtless, something there is he has to plead in excuse and extenuation of his fault. Whatsoever it be, let it be produced, and weighed in the balance of right reason;

Valeat quantum valere potest: Let it have its due value and consideration. And could I imagine anything more likely to be their inducements, than what I shall here mention, I would not conceal them. There are only four things, that can fall within the compass of my imagination, pleaded by them, when seriously charged with the evil of the fact.

(i) Some of them will happily tell us, that they would not swear as they do, if they could gain credit to what they say without it; but the incredulity of others, provokes them to add so many oaths to their single affirmations.

(ii) Others of them will tell us, they only swear in their passion, when provoked by injuries received from others; and if men did not wrong them, they would not wrong God as they do.

(iii) Some will plead, that swearing is become modish, the badge and character

of a gentleman; that it gives them reputation among men of their own rank and
quality; and that they shall be looked upon
as sneaking fools, unfit for the company of
gentlemen, if they could not discourse with
them in this dialect.

(iv) And some will confess the practice
is evil; but that they have gotten such an ill
habit, and the sin is become so customary
with them, that many times they know not
whether they swear or not.

I cannot imagine, nor (I think) they
themselves, what else is pleadable in excuse,
or extenuation of this horrid sin: let these
that are produced, have a fair trial at the
bar of reason; and carry yourselves towards
this sin for ever hereafter, according to that
righteous verdict you yourselves shall be
forced to pass upon it.

6. To begin with the first plea. You say, you would not swear as you do, could you gain credit to your words without it.

Weigh this question in the upright balance of your own reason, whether any wise or sober man in the world, will find himself ever the more obliged to believe what you say, by the addition of blasphemous oaths and imprecations, to your plain and simple affirmations or negations. I cannot think, that you yourselves would give the more credit to any man, that should profess his sincerity to you, by finding him, in that his very profession, false and treacherous to his God. Say, reason, do not you take this for a sure truth; that he who makes no conscience of being true to God, will never make much conscience of being false to men? For what is that which gives any man's words reputation among wise and sober men, but the supposition of his integrity, and conscientious fear of his deceit and guile? Take away that, and with it you take away the credibility of all his reports and affirmations.

If I look upon the person that speaks, as a man of integrity and conscientious tenderness, I have a sufficient ordinary security of the truth of what he saith. But if I look upon him as a man of a prostitute and seared conscience, that dares venture upon any sin; a man, in whom there is no awe of God, to produce veracity in his words; then my reason presently concludes, that where there is no truth, there ought to be no trust: for truth is the very ground-work and foundation of trust.

Now, what truth can we suppose to be left in that man, that sticks not, upon any trivial occasion, to break asunder all the obligations of a creature to his Creator, together with all the bonds of kindness, his great and best benefactor has bound him withal; and without any the least injury he can pretend his God has done him, to fly in his very face with the most insultingly rude language? Can we suppose any truth to be in, or any trust to be due to such a man as this?

Good men and bad are thus distinguished from each other: 'Him that sweareth, and he that feareth an oath' (*Eccles.* 9:2). A conscientious man is so afraid of an oath, that he would rather choose to die, than swear some kind of oaths: and though he be satisfied of the lawfulness of an oath in general, and of the matter of an oath he swears in particular; yet an holy awe and fear of God fills his heart, when he swears lawfully and necessarily, lest he should fail in the manner of it, by not giving that due reverence to the name of God, which so sacred and solemn an action requires.

But from profane swearing, and blaspheming the name of God, every man's reason may justly and plainly infer this conclusion; that the fear of God, is not in that man's heart. And where there is no fear of God, what truth can be supposed in him; or what trust can be due to his words or oaths? But the more he swears, still the less reason all wise men have to believe him. And I am sure, the credulity of fools adds little reputation to him. This plea therefore, for profane swearing, is altogether shamed, baffled, and cashiered, by the common reason of mankind.

7. *Call therefore to the bar of reason the second plea, or apology, for profane swearing.*

You say, you swear not, unless provoked by injuries men have done you.

This is so weak a plea for so great a sin, that I wonder men are not ashamed to bring it into the court of reason. This is the true sense, and strength of it: my enemy has abused me; therefore I will avenge the wrong my enemy has done me, upon my best friend and benefactor.

I challenge you to give but the colour, or shadow of sound reason, why, upon any abuse you have received from men, you should fall so injuriously upon the name of God, who never abused or injured you, since he gave you a being, but has always done you good. Tell me, man, (if you have the reason of a man in you) what wrong has God done you? Wherein has he injured you, that you thus wreak your revenge upon him? If an enemy has affronted you, reason would tell you, you ought not to take revenge for it, upon your friend, and best benefactor. Have you none but God to abuse, when men abuse and injure you? Can your reason approve of and allow such an action as this? Satan instigates the corruptions of men to injure you; and you fly in the face of God for it, whose laws severely prohibit such actions, and will avenge the injuries done unto him.

Speak no more therefore for ever, in the way of excusing the horrid sinfulness of this fact against God, upon the account of injuries done you by your fellow creature. The case is plainly determined, and cast over the bar of reason with contempt and abhorrence.

8. *Come we next to your third excuse, or plea; that swearing is become modish [fashionable], and gives you a great reputation among men of your own rank and quality; and that you shall be looked upon as sneaking fellows, unfit for the society of gentlemen, if you did not discourse with them in their own dialect.*

This apology for sin is of no late date: Salvian mentions it as far back as his own time: profane persons then thus pleaded for themselves, that they were compelled to be evil, lest they should be accounted vile. Whether there be any weight in this apology for swearing, will quickly appear, now it is to be laid in the balance of true reason.

(1) And first of all, let us consider what makes a true gentleman; and whether profane swearing have any place in his true

character and description. A gentleman, is one that springs from famous and renowned ancestors, and degenerates not from their probity and honour. This is the man, whom the Latins call *generosus,* and we, a gentleman: because we suppose a man of such an extraction and education, more gentle, affable, and condescending to inferiors, and to keep a stricter government over his tongue and passions, than the rude plebians [common people] usually do. Upon this account, the poet rightly observes,

Quo major est quisquis, magis est placabilis ira,
Et facilis motus mens generosa capit.

Men of genteel extraction and education, are persons, whose passions are supposed to move more gently than other men's: and if at any time they be moved disorderly, yet are they more placable, and sooner reduced, than those of sordid and baser spirits are.

It is virtue which raises and ennobles families at first; for *omnis sanguis concolor:* all human blood is derived from, and equally tainted by Adam. Nobler, and baser blood, is an after-difference, made by virtue and vice among men. And as virtue first ennobled, and raised some families above others, so it will still continue the line of honour in their posterity: and as their virtues shall increase, so will their honour proportionably do.

The case truly and plainly standing thus; it is morally impossible to make debauchery the proper badge and character of gentility. For men of eminency (above the vulgar) are more obliged than they, to shun all base and sordid actions: and as their honour increases, so do their obligations to temperance and sobriety increase, and strengthen upon them proportionably.

It was therefore a right and rational observation of Jerome: 'I see nothing desirable in nobility, (says he) but this; that such men are bound by a certain kind of necessity, not to degenerate from, or stain the glory and honour of their renowned ancestors.' And the reason is strong and evident: for virtue being that which first differenced their blood from others, they are obliged, by all the value they have for the honour of their blood and families, to shun those vices which stain that honour and dignity.

And what vice can dishonour and debase them more than profane swearing? For if the arms of many noble families have been reversed for treason against the king; it is irrational to imagine, that treason against the King of kings, should add a new mark of honour: and what is blasphemy but treason against God?

It is plain then, from the true rise and character of a gentleman, profane swearing neither first raised, nor can preserve and continue, but rather blots and exposes their reputation and honour.

(2) Though I am most willing to pay a becoming deference to all persons of noble and genteel extraction, yet, in faithfulness to their true honour, I am here obliged to say, (and in saying it, I can offend no man who has a true sense of honour) that their natural descent can never give them so much honour, as the vices I am here censuring will reflect ignominy and dishonour upon him.

To be a slave of Satan, and your own lusts, is such a mark of infamy, as all the honourable and illustrious titles in the world can never cover. It is better to rise by virtue to honour, from contemptible parents, than by vice and profaneness, to grow contemptible from honourable parents. It is your honour to have many servants at your command, obsequiously attending a nod of your head, or a beck of your finger: but ask your own reason, gentlemen, whether it be not a greater dishonour, for you to attend as obsequiously yourselves upon every beck and nod of Satan and your own lusts?

Were your natural birth once ennobled by the new birth, you would be more than three-times honourable, grace would make you more illustrious than your natural extraction does, or can do. Or if morality (which is far inferior to that honour, and for which heathens themselves have been renowned in the Pagan world) did but adorn and beautify your conversations; though it cannot entitle you to heaven, or secure to you the glory of the world to come; yet it would make you shine in the eyes of men in this world, and taking its advantage from your honourable extraction, make you differ from persons of an inferior rank, as stars of greater magnitude and lustre. I hope, gentlemen valuing themselves upon their honour, will not be offended at a sharper invective than this, against those vices that darken and eclipse their honour, both in the eyes of God, as well as in the judgment of all wise and good men.

(3) Suppose what you say to be true, that some profane gentlemen should scoff

and deride you, for your sober way of life, and decorous language, (things which ought to be inseparable from true gentility) I would in this case appeal to your own reason, why you should not enjoy your own pleasure in as full latitude and liberty, as they do theirs?—they delight in the dialect of devils; you, in pure and inoffensive language. If they will drink the puddled waters, and you refuse them for the pure crystal streams; you have, to be sure, as much reason (and a thousand times more) to assert your liberty to be virtuous, than they have (or can pretend to have) a privilege to be vicious.

And if they will be offended with you for this, their offence is groundless in themselves, and will be greatly advantageous to you. For you need not doubt but you may find better company than theirs anywhere on this side of hell.

I remember that rational and excellent apology, which Tertullian made for the Christians in his time against the Gentiles: 'Wherein (said he) do we offend you, if we will not partake with you in your delights! If we sustain any damage by such a refusal, the injury can only be our own: we reject your pleasures, and you are not delighted with ours.'

You will show yourselves true and worthy gentlemen, in abandoning and rejecting (upon so noble an account as this) all further unnecessary society with such gentile-men; for so they deserve to be called, rather than gentlemen. They boast, indeed the honour of their blood, whilst they trample the precious and invaluable blood of Christ under their feet: they boast their eminency above the vulgar, whilst meantime they work evil against him who set them there.

I am sure there is not a devil in hell, but is by nature of a more honourable and illustrious house, than the proudest blasphemers. They are angels by nature, though devils by practice. They have little reason to boast of their original excellency, which now aggravates their misery. Sin darkened their lustre, degraded them from their natural dignity; and so it will do theirs also, that imitate devils in their blasphemy and malignity against God.

(4) It may as easily be proved as asserted, that to make cursing, swearing, and blaspheming, the badges and characteristic marks of a true gentleman, is the foulest blot and mark of infamy, which the

malice of their enemies can devise to put into their reputations; and such an affront, as ought to be highly resented by all true gentlemen.

Should the most malicious enemy you have in the world, employ an herald to devise a mark of infamy for your coats of arms, to make you ridiculous, and a byword among the people; he could never dishonour you at that rate, you this way dishonour yourselves.

For if debauchery be both asserted and allowed to be the true badge of gentility, then your own reason will infer, that all the ancient epithets of gentility ought thereupon to be altered. And would those gentlemen, do you think, take it well, to have the titles, and epithets of ingenious, worthy, honourable, and noble, changed into cursing, swearing, damning, blaspheming gentlemen? You cannot but see the inconsistency of both. If, therefore, you will adopt and wear the latter, you must either give up and renounce the former, or try to make the former consistent with the latter, which I am sure the most ingenious among you will find an hard task to do.

(5) I humbly beg leave to propound one plain blunt question to you, gentlemen. The matter of it is too rational to be rejected, and let that make atonement for the blunt manner of its proposal. And the question is this:

Question. *Whether your reason and conscience be fully satisfied, that when you die (as you know you shortly must,) you shall then appear before the judgment-seat of God, in the quality and character of gentlemen? Do you verily think you shall find the more favour there, for the sake of your noble descent, and honourable extraction, or that your gentility shall make an atonement for all your impiety?*

I am persuaded, gentlemen, you do not; you cannot think so. You know you must appear before that God, with whom there is no respect of persons; a God that will certainly damn the impenitent blasphemer. The man must assuredly go to hell (1 *Cor.* 6:9-10). And if the man be damned, certainly the gentleman is in a bad case.

9. *There is but one plea more; and that as silly and irrational as any of the former: and that is, the custom and habit of swearing, which you say is hard to be broken. This sin is become so customary to you, that now you scarce note or observe it in yourselves.*

That there may be truth in the matter of this plea, I neither deny nor doubt; but that it is a rational and allowable plea, will never be granted by your own reason. The thing you say may be true; for we sometimes find, that when you are taxed for swearing, you will presently swear that you did not swear; and curse him to his face, that accuses you for cursing.

But pray, gentlemen, make your own reason judge, whether custom be a valid and allowed plea for profane swearing and cursing. Say, reason, will you allow that one of the highest aggravations of sin, is pleadable in your court for the excuse and extenuation of it? Will you give it under your hand, that the man is the less guilty, because the more wicked? Dare you to warrant it that God will take the less notice of the wrongs men do him, because they are used and accustomed so to wrong and abuse him every hour in the day? If your reason can allow and warrant this, I must say it is different, yea, and opposite to the common reason of mankind.

Say not, I make my own reason the rule and standard of yours, or other men's. For I argue here (as I have done all along before) upon the common topics and maxims of reason, generally allowed all the world over by mankind. If a practice be evil, the oftener it is repeated, the more still it is aggravated.

To be plain and faithful with you gentlemen, if it be your custom to blaspheme, it is God's custom to damn blasphemers. If you use to be drunken and unclean, God uses to punish drunkards and adulterers (if

impenitent and unreformed) with his everlasting wrath.

And when you are cited (as shortly
you must be) before the awful tribunal of
the great, the just, and the terrible God,
ask but yourselves, whether such a plea as
this, be like to excuse in whole, or in part,
and take off the heinousness of these horrid
impieties? Will your profane oaths, and
direful execrations and imprecations, be
excused in the least degree, by telling him,
Lord, I was so accustomed to blaspheme
your name; cursing, swearing, and damning, were so familiar language in my lips
from day to day, that I had quite lost the
sense of the action, as well as of the evil
thereof; and therefore, Lord, pity, spare and
have mercy on me: O damn not my soul to
your everlasting wrath. For though I have

imprecated it upon myself, yet frequent custom at length distinguished all my sense and conscience of the evil thereof, till at length I could play with a direful imprecation as an harmless thing; nay, thought it an ornament and grace to my speech, a gallant expression of the times and places I lived in.

Is not this as good a plea, and not a jot better than that of a criminal upon his trial for life and death, when theft or robbery have been evidently and substantially proved against him, and the judge demands, What he has to say for himself, why sentence of death should not pass upon him? Mercy, my Lord, mercy, he cries! for I have been so used and accustomed to filching and thieving from my youth up, that for some years before I was apprehended, every one's goods and cattle seemed to me to look like my own; so that I scarce knew when I stole, and when I did not.

And thus, gentlemen, you have heard a fair trial of the sin of profane swearing, and imprecations of damnation; and you have heard the verdict of your own reason and conscience upon the case. The Lord help you to break off and reform that sin, for which there is not one word of apology or excuse now left in your mouths.

Let me close all I have to say upon this head, with one plain question: Do you think you must die, or live here for ever, as you now do? If you are convinced (as all the living are supposed to be) that you must die, do you desire an easy and comfortable, or a painful and terrible death? I presume there is no man living, that is convinced he must die, but desires naturally and rationally an εὐθανασίαν [euthanasian], as easy and comfortable a dissolution as may be.

If so, I appeal to your reason, whether profane swearing and blaspheming the name of God, be a proper rational way to obtain peace and comfort at death? With what hope or encouragement can those tongues of yours cry at death, Lord, have mercy upon me, which have profaned that name, and imprecated damnation from him, till you come into your last extremities, which convinced you, you could live no longer.

It is a serious question, and well worth a cool and solemn debate in your own reasons and consciences.

Some of you are more immediately exposed to the dangers of death than others, readily to be disbanded by a bullet. If you fall, you must either fall considerately, or inconsiderately. If inconsiderately, and without any sense or conscience of this horrid guilt, you die impenitently, and consequently desperately and miserably. If considerately, and with awakened consciences, I demand, whether such guilt as this will not roar louder than the peals and volleys of those great and small guns do which breathe destruction upon you, and round about you?

I have done my message plainly and faithfully to the very face of your reason and conscience; and if for my faithfulness and zeal, both for God's honour and yours, I am rewarded with your curses; yet, if you would forbear to blaspheme and rend in pieces the name of God, I shall not much regard the obloquy and reproach my name shall undergo and suffer upon that account: but I expect from you better fruit than this.

OTHER BOOKS IN THE
POCKET PURITANS
SERIES

If you enjoyed reading this little book then you may be interested to know that the Banner of Truth Trust also publishes the six-volume set of Flavel's *Works* (ISBN: 978 0 85151 060 6, approximately 600 pp. per volume, clothbound), and Flavel's *The Mystery of Providence* (ISBN: 978 0 85151 104 7, 224 pp. in the Puritan Paperback series).

For more details of these and all other Banner of Truth titles, please visit our website:

www.banneroftruth.co.uk

THE BANNER OF TRUTH TRUST

3 Murrayfield Road, Edinburgh EH12 6EL UK

P O Box 621, Carlisle, Philadelphia 17013, USA

www.banneroftruth.co.uk